A First Treasury of
NURSERY RHYMES

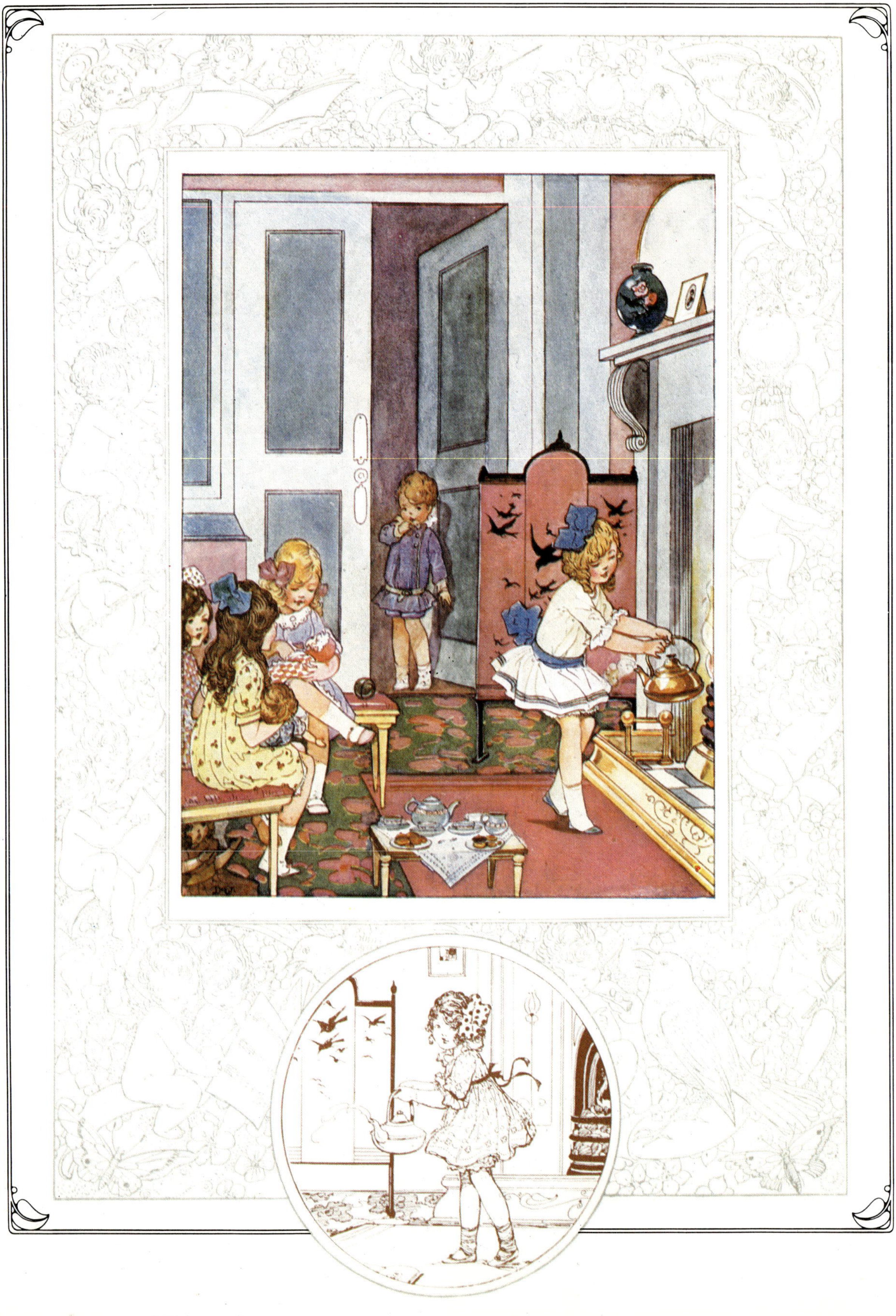

A First Treasury of
NURSERY RHYMES
With Classic Illustrations

Edited by Michael Foss

MACMILLAN CHILDREN'S BOOKS

Acknowledgments

The editor and publishers would like to thank the following people for giving permission to include in this anthology material which is in their copyright. The publishers have made every effort to trace copyright holders. If we have inadvertently omitted to acknowledge anyone we should be most grateful if this could be brought to our attention for correction at the earliest opportunity.

George Allen and Unwin for the poems from *Collected Works* by Arthur Waley.
Jonathan Cape Ltd., Holt Rinehart Winston and the author's estate for the poem by Robert Frost.
Doubleday and Co. Inc. for the poem by Theodore Roethke.
Little Brown and Co. Inc. for the poems by Ogden Nash.
Ian Seraillier for his poem.

Copyright © Michael O'Mara Books Ltd 1985

Copyright © Introduction Michael Foss 1985

All rights reserved. No reproduction, copy or transmission of this publication may be made without written permission. No paragraph of this publication may be reproduced, copied or transmitted save with written permission or in accordance with the provisions of the Copyright Act 1956 (as amended). Any person who does any unauthorised act in relation to this publication may be liable to criminal prosecution and civil claims for damages.

First published 1985 by Michael O'Mara Books Ltd
Designed by Martin Bristow

Picturemac edition published 1987 by
Macmillan Children's Books
A division of Macmillan Publishers Limited
London and Basingstoke
Associated companies throughout the world

British Library Cataloguing in Publication Data
[A Treasury of nursery rhymes]. A First treasury of nursery rhymes:
with classic illustrations.——(Picturemac).
Vol. 1
1. Nursery rhymes, English
I. Foss, Michael
398'.8   PZ8.3

ISBN 0-333-45618-1

Printed in Spain

Contents

Introduction 7

Beginnings 9

Beasts and Other Animals 31

Have Fun! 51

Take Heed! 71

Index of First Lines 80

Index of Artists 80

Introduction

In Boston, Massachusetts, in the late 17th century, there was said to be a formidable goodwife by the name of Mistress Elizabeth Goose. In her time sixteen children had clung to her skirts, a noisy little army which she soothed and entertained with a stream of nursery rhymes drawn up from her voluminous memory. Her son-in-law, doubly impressed by the depth of her memory and by the joyful effects of the rhymes on the children, set them down and called the book *Mother Goose's Melodies for Children*. Alas, this story is an invention, put about in the 19th century to give a local home and explanation to a more international character: the Boston housewife was in reality the American personification of the old German *Fru Gosen*, the French *Mère Oye* and the English *Mother Goose*.

But this pleasant little American tale is a sign that 'Mother Goose' with her store of children's verse is a substantial, even a necessary figure in the childhood of all nations. She had been around for so long and had fitted so comfortably into tradition, all countries were convinced they owned her. In fact, 'Mother Goose' is every mother (and father too!) of every child everywhere. She is the fond nurse who calms, delights, instructs and corrects her child with a happy and varied body of verse which has proved so powerful and effective that it is repeated and extended in every generation. Here, then, is a collection for our age.

But what *is* a nursery rhyme? We are accustomed to think of it as one of the simple verses that appeared in the many early volumes of *Mother Goose*. We now know, however, that the rhymes for those books were drawn from a thousand different sources – from plays, chap-books, broadsheets, moral pamphlets, popular songs, as well as from oral tradition; and the works of poets everywhere, alive and dead, were not neglected. Indeed, we may say that a nursery rhyme is nothing more or less than a verse, from whatever source, that enters into the particular imaginative world of the child. In this world, reality is insecure and changeable, things are seen simple and stark, the colours are bold, joy and terror are not far apart, and nonsense is just as good as sense. It is a world into which an old blind fiddler may enter as easily as a Shakespeare.

The rhymes in this book – verses as various and divergent as those that made up the original *Mother Goose* – are the ancient and modern poetry of the child's world.

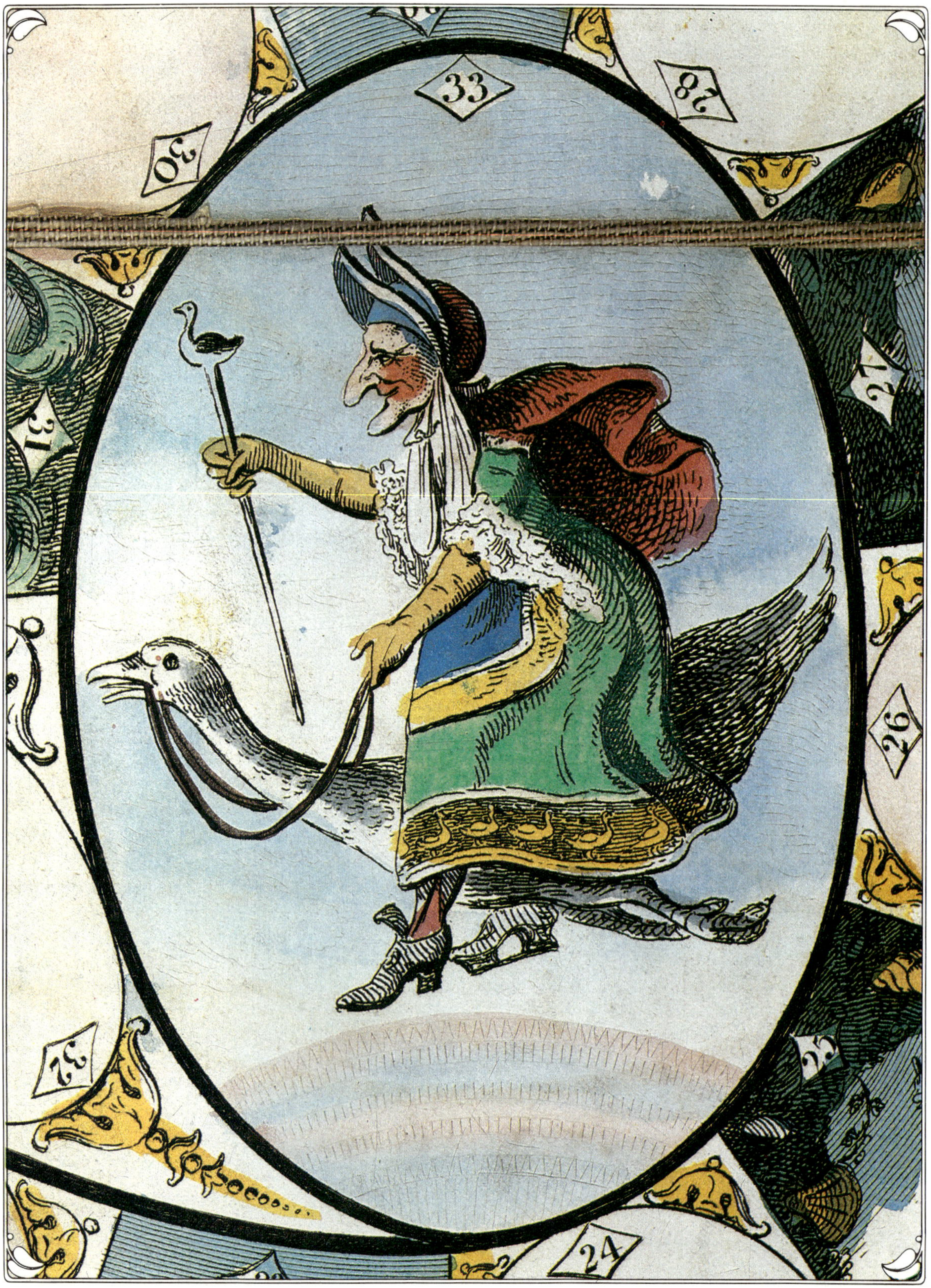
33
30
28
27
31
26
32
24

Beginnings

Sleep, baby, sleep,
Thy father guards the sheep;
Thy mother shakes the dreamland tree
And from it fall sweet dreams for thee,
Sleep, baby, sleep.

I'm so sorry for old Adam,
  Just as sorry as can be;
For he never had no mammy
  For to hold him on her knee.

For he never had no childhood,
  Playin' round the cabin door,
And he never had no daddy
  For to tell him all he know.

And I've always had the feelin'
  He'd a let that apple be,
If he'd only had a mammy
  For to hold him on her knee.

We dance round in a ring and suppose,
But the Secret sits in the middle and knows.

What is there hid in the heart of a rose,
        Mother-mine?
Ah, who knows, who knows, who knows?
A Man that died on a lonely hill
May tell you, perhaps, but none other will,
        Little child.

What does it take to make a rose,
        Mother-mine?
The God that died to make it knows
It takes the world's eternal wars,
It takes the moon and all the stars,
It takes the might of heaven and hell
And the everlasting Love as well,
        Little child.

I'm goin' away for to stay a little while,
But I'm comin' back if I go ten thousand miles.
Oh, who will tie your shoes?
And who will glove your hands?
And who will kiss your ruby lips when I am gone?

Oh, it's pappy'll tie my shoes,
And mammy'll glove my hands,
And you will kiss my ruby lips when you come back!

Oh, he's gone, he's gone away,
For to stay a little while,
But he's comin' back if he goes ten thousand miles.

Chicken in the bread-pan,
Pickin' up the dough;
Granny will your dog bite?
No, child, no.

All I need to make me happy,
Two little boys to call me pappy,
One named Biscuit t'other named Gravy,
If I had another I'd call him Davy.

There was an Old Woman
Lived under a hill,
And if she isn't gone
She lives there still.

Baked apples she sold
And cranberry pies,
And she's the old woman
That never told lies.

Young lambs to sell.
Young lambs to sell.
If I'd as much money as I can tell,
I never would cry – Young lambs to sell.

London Bridge is falling down,
Falling down, falling down,
London Bridge is falling down,
My fair lady.

Build it up with wood and clay,
Wood and clay, wood and clay,
Build it up with wood and clay,
My fair lady.

Build it up with bricks and mortar,
Bricks and mortar, bricks and mortar,
Build it up with bricks and mortar,
My fair lady.

Bricks and mortar will not stay,
Will not stay, will not stay,
Bricks and mortar will not stay,
My fair lady.

Build it up with iron and steel,
Iron and steel, iron and steel,
Build it up with iron and steel,
My fair lady.

Iron and steel will bend and bow,
Bend and bow, bend and bow,
Iron and steel will bend and bow,
My fair lady.

Build it up with silver and gold,
Silver and gold, silver and gold,
Build it up with silver and gold,
My fair lady.

Silver and gold will be stolen away,
Stolen away, stolen away,
Silver and gold will be stolen away,
My fair lady.

Set a man to watch all night,
Watch all night, watch all night,
Set a man to watch all night,
My fair lady.

Suppose the man should fall asleep,
Fall asleep, fall asleep,
Suppose the man should fall asleep,
My fair lady.

Give him a pipe to smoke all night,
Smoke all night, smoke all night,
Give him a pipe to smoke all night,
My fair lady.

I brought my love a cherry that has no stone,
I brought my love a chicken that has no bone,
I told my love a story that has no end,
I brought my love a baby and no crying.

How can there be a cherry that has no stone?
How can there be a chicken that has no bone?
How can there be a story that has no end?
How can there be a baby and no crying?

A cherry when it's blooming, it has no stone;
A chicken in the egg, it has no bone;
The story of our love shall have no end;
A baby when it's sleeping does no crying.

Three children sliding on the ice,
    Upon a summer's day,
As it fell out, they all fell in,
    The rest they ran away.

Now had these children been at home,
    Or sliding on dry ground,
Ten thousand pounds to one penny
    They had not all been drowned.

You parents all that children have,
    And you that have got none,
If you would have them safe abroad,
    Pray keep them safe at home.

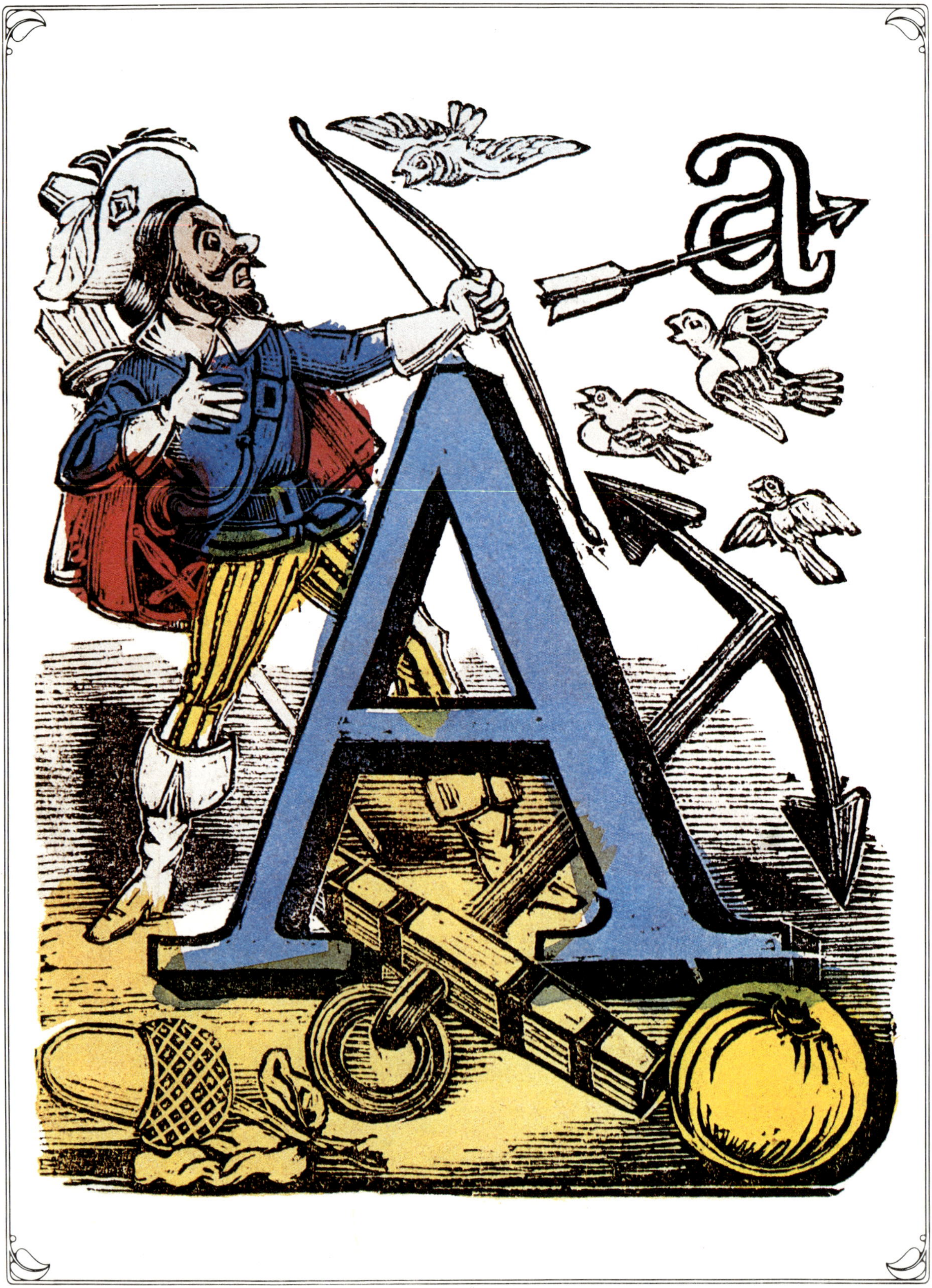

A tumbled down, and hurt his Arm, against a bit of wood.

B said, 'My Boy, O! do not cry; it cannot do you good!'

C said, 'A Cup of Coffee hot can't do you any harm.'

D said, 'A Doctor should be fetched, and he would cure the arm.'

E said, 'An Egg beat up with milk would quickly make him feel well.'

F said, 'A Fish, if broiled, might cure, if only by the smell.'

G said, 'Green Gooseberry fool, the best of cures I hold.'

H said, 'His Hat should be kept on, to keep him from the cold.'

I said, 'Some Ice upon his head will make him better soon.'

J said, 'Some Jam, if spread on bread, or given in a spoon!'

K said, 'A Kangaroo is here, – this picture let him see.'

L said, 'A Lamp pray keep alight, to make some barley tea.'

M said, 'A Mulberry or two might give him satisfaction.'

N said, 'Some Nuts, if rolled about, might be a slight attraction.'

O said, 'An Owl might make him laugh, if only it would wink.'

P said, 'Some Poetry might be read aloud, to make him think.'

Q said, 'A Quince I recommend, – a Quince, or else a Quail.'

R said, 'Some Rats might make him move, if fastened by their tail.'

S said, 'A Song should now be sung, in hopes to make him laugh!'

T said, 'A Turnip might avail, if sliced or cut in half!'

U said, 'An Urn, with water hot, placed underneath his chin.'

V said, 'I'll stand upon a chair, and play a Violin.

W said, 'Some Whisky-Whizzgigs fetch, some marbles and a ball!'

X said, 'Some double XX ale would be the best of all.'

Y said, 'Some Yeast mixed up with salt would make a perfect plaster!'

Z said, 'Here is a box of Zinc! Get in, my little master!

'We'll shut you up! We'll nail you down! We will, my little master!

'We think we've all heard quite enough of this your sad disaster!'

23

Ring-a-ring o' roses,
A pocket full of posies,
A-tishoo, a-tishoo!
We all fall down.

Hickory, dickory, dock,
The mouse ran up the clock.
The clock struck one,
The mouse ran down,
Hickory, dickory, dock

Baa, baa, black sheep
Have you any wool?
Yes sir, yes sir,
Three bags full;
One for the master,
And one for the dame,
And one for the little boy
Who lives down the lane.

Girls are dandy,
Made of candy:
That's what little girls are made of.
Boys are rotten,
Made of cotton:
That's what little boys are made of.

Flies in the buttermilk, two by two,
If you can't get a red-bird, a blue-bird'll do.
I've lost my girl, now what'll I do?
I'll get another, a better one too.
Pa's got a shotgun, Number 32.
Hurry up slowpoke, do, do, do.
My little girl wears a No 9 shoe,
When I go a-courting, I take two.
Gone again, now what'll I do?
I'll get another, sweeter than you.
He's got big feet, and awkward too.
Kitten in the haymow, mew, mew, mew.
I'll get her back in spite of you.
We'll keep it up 'til half past two.
One old boot and a rundown shoe.
Stole my partner, skip to my Lou.
Skip to my Lou, skip to my Lou,
Skip to my Lou, my darling.

Little Jack Horner
Sat in the corner,
Eating a Christmas pie;
He put in a thumb,
And pulled out a plum,
And said, What a good boy am I.

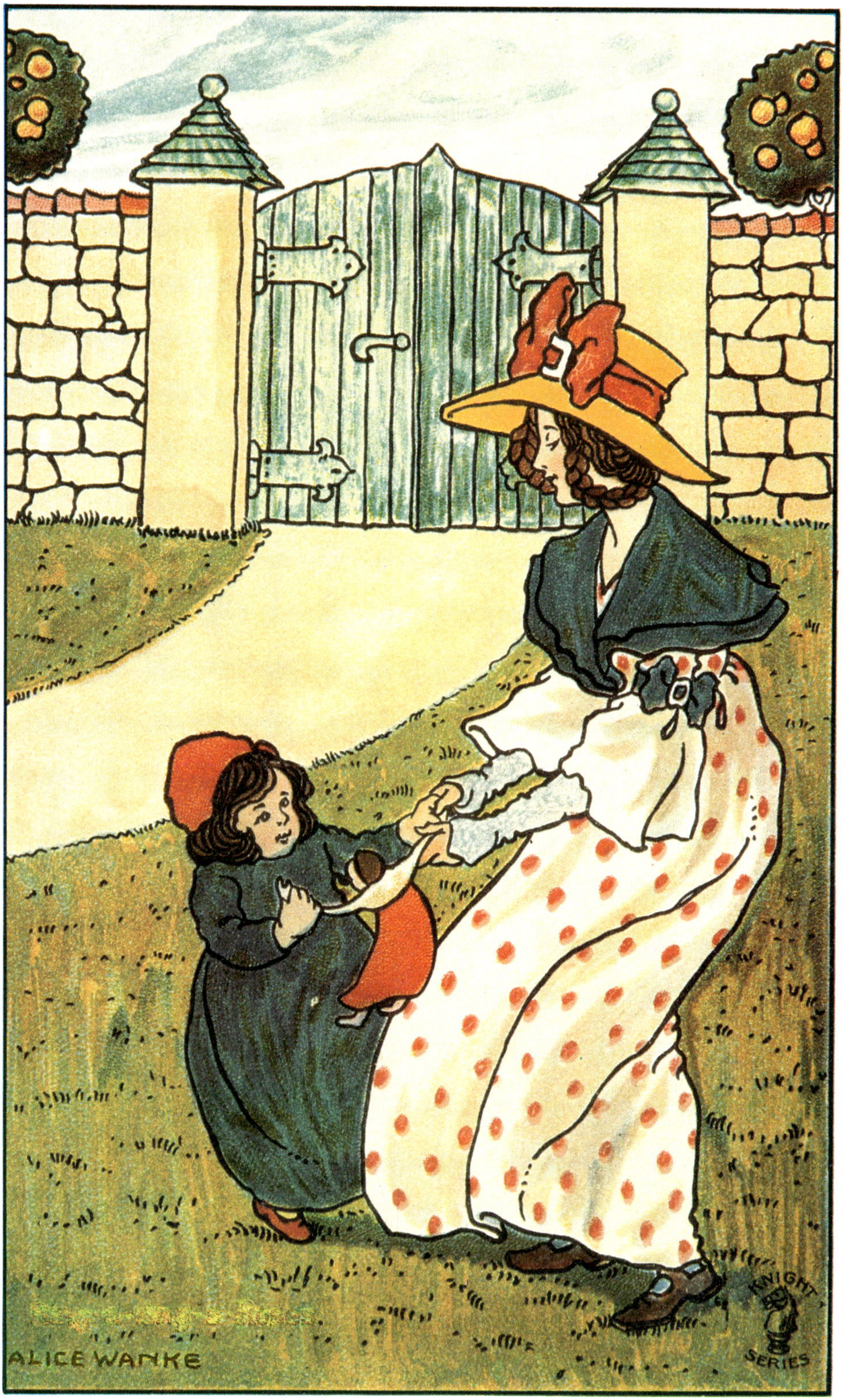
ALICE WANKE
KNIGHT
SERIES

BAA, BAA! BLACK SHEEP

Beasts and Other Animals

Massah had an old black mule,
His name was Simon Slick,
The only mule with screamin' eyes,
An' how that mule could kick.

He kicked the feathers from the goose,
He broke the elephant's back,
He stopped the Texas railroad train
An' he kicked it off the track.

The Lord made an elephant,
He made him stout;
The first thing he made
Was the elephant's snout.

He made his snout nigh long as a rail,
The next thing he made was the elephant's tail;
He made his tail to fan the flies,
The next thing he made was the elephant's eyes.

He made his eyes to see green trees,
The next thing he made was the elephant's knees.
Oh, elephant, you shall be free,
Oh, elephant, you shall be free,
When the good Lord sets you free.

Five little monkeys walked along the shore;
One went a-sailing,
Then there were four.
Four little monkeys climbed up a tree;
One of them tumbled down,
Then there were three.
Three little monkeys found a pot of glue;
One got stuck in it,
Then there were two.
Two little monkeys found a currant bun;
One ran away with it,
Then there was one.
One little monkey cried all afternoon,
So they put him in an aeroplane
And sent him to the moon.

I dreamed that my horse had wings and could fly,
I jumped on my horse and rode to the sky.
The man in the moon was out that night,
He laughed long and loud when I pranced into sight.

My Mammy was a wall-eyed goat,
My Old Man was an ass,
I feed myself off leather boots
And dynamite and grass.
For I'm a mule, a long-eared fool
And I ain't never been to school
   Hee-hee-haw.

Three mice went into a hole to spin,
Puss passed by and she peeped in:
'What are you doing, my little men?'
'Weaving coats for gentlemen.'
'Please let me come in to wind off your thread.'
'Oh no, Mistress Pussy, you'll bite off our heads.'

Says Puss: 'You look so wondrous wise,
I like your whiskers and bright black eyes,
Your house is the nicest house I see,
I think there is room for you and me.'
The mice were so pleased that they opened the door,
And pussy soon laid them all dead on the floor.

I WISH I were a
Elephantiaphus
And I could pick off the coconuts with my nose.
But, oh! I am not,
(Alas! I cannot be)
An Elephanti-
Elephantiaphus.
But I'm a cockroach
And I'm a water-bug,
I can crawl around and hide behind the sink.

I wish I were a
Rhinoscereeacus
And could wear an ivory toothpick in my nose.
But, oh! I am not,
(Alas, I cannot be)
A Rhinoscori-
Rhinoscereeacus.
But I'm a beetle
And I'm a pumpkin-bug,
I can buzz and bang my head against the wall.

I wish I were a
Hippopopotamus
And could swim the Tigris and broad Gangés.
But, oh! I am not,
(Alas! I cannot be)
A hippopopo-
Hippopopotamus.
But I'm a grasshopper
And I'm a katydid,
I can play the fiddle with my left hind-leg.

I wish I were a
Levileviathan
And had seven hundred knuckles in my spine.
But, oh! I am not,
(Alas! I cannot be)
A Levi-ikey-
A Levi-ikey-mo.
But I'm a firefly
And I'm a lightning-bug,
I can light cheroots and gaspers with my tail.

'Who's that tickling my back?' said the wall.
'Me,' said a small
Caterpillar. 'I'm learning
To crawl.'

The panther is like a leopard,
Except it hasn't been peppered.
Should you behold a panther crouch,
Prepare to say Ouch.
Better yet, if called by a panther,
Don't anther.

A hungry fox one day did spy,
Some nice ripe grapes that hung so high,
And as they hung they seemed to say
To him who underneath did stay,
'If you can fetch me down you may.'

The fox his patience nearly lost,
With expectations baulked and crossed,
He licked his lips for near an hour,
Till he found the prize beyond his power,
Then he went, and swore the grapes were sour!

There was a little turtle.
He lived in a box.
He swam in a puddle.
He climbed on the rocks.

He snapped at a mosquito
He snapped at a flea.
He snapped at a minnow.
And he snapped at me.

He caught the mosquito.
He caught the flea.
He caught the minnow.
But he didn't catch me.

Four and twenty tailor lads
Were fighting with a slug,
'Hallo, sirs,' said one of them,
'Just hold him by the lug.'
But the beastie from his shell came out,
And shook his fearsome head,
'Run, run, my tailors bold,
Or we will all be dead.'

My sweetheart's a mule in the mines,
I drive her without reins or lines,
   On the bumper I sit,
   I chew and I spit
All over my sweetheart's behind.

Ol Mr Rabbit
You've got a mighty habit
Of jumping in the garden
And eating all my cabbage.

Daddy shot a bear,
Daddy shot a bear,
Shot him through the keyhole,
And he never touched a hair.

Our dog Fred
Et the bread.

Our dog Dash
Et the hash.

Our dog Pete
Et the meat

Our dog Davy
Et the gravy.

Our dog Toffy
Et the coffee.

Our dog Jake
Et the cake.

Our dog Trip
Et the dip.

And – the worst
From the first, –

Our dog Fido
Et the pie-dough.

Old Mistress McShuttle
Lived in a coal-scuttle
Along with her dog and her cat.
What they ate I can't tell,
But 'tis known very well
That not one of the party was fat.

Old Mistress McShuttle
Scoured out her coal-scuttle
And washed both her dog and her cat.
The cat scratched her nose,
So they both came to hard blows,
And who was the gainer by that?

Little Betty Winkle she had a pig,
It was a little pig and not very big;
When he was alive he lived in clover,
But now he's dead and that's all over.
Johnny Winkle, he sat down and cried,
Betty Winkle, she lay down and died;
So there's an end of one, two and three,
Johnny, Betty and little Piggie Wiggie.

Mister Rabbit, Mister Rabbit, your ears mighty long,
Yes, my Lawd, they're put on wrong.

Mister Rabbit, Mister Rabbit, your coat mighty grey,
Yes, my Lawd, 'twas made that way.

Mister Rabbit, Mister Rabbit, your feet mighty red,
Yes, my Lawd, I'm almost dead.

Mister Rabbit, Mister Rabbit, your tail mighty white,
Yes, my Lawd, I'm a-getting out of sight.

Mister Rabbit, Mister Rabbit, you look mighty thin,
Yes, my Lawd, been cutting through the wind.

Every little soul must shine, shine shine,
Every little soul must shine, shine, shine.

The Kitty-Cat Bird, he sat on a Fence.
Said the Wren, your Song isn't worth 10¢.
You're a Fake, you're a Fraud, you're a Hor-rid Pretense!
  – Said the Wren to the Kitty-Cat Bird.

You've too many tunes, and none of them Good:
I wish you would act like a bird really should,
Or stay by yourself down deep in the wood,
  – Said the Wren to the Kitty-Cat Bird.

You mew like a Cat, you grate like a Jay:
You squeak like a Mouse that's lost in the Hay,
I wouldn't be You for even a day,
  – Said the Wren to the Kitty-Cat Bird.

The Kitty-Cat Bird, he moped and he cried.
Then a real cat came with a Mouth so Wide,
That the Kitty-Cat Bird just hopped inside;
'At last I'm myself!' – and he up and died
  – Did the Kitty – the Kitty-Cat Bird.

You'd better not laugh; and don't say, 'Pooh!'
Until you have thought this Sad Tale through:
Be sure that whatever you are is you
  – Or you'll end like the Kitty-Cat Bird.

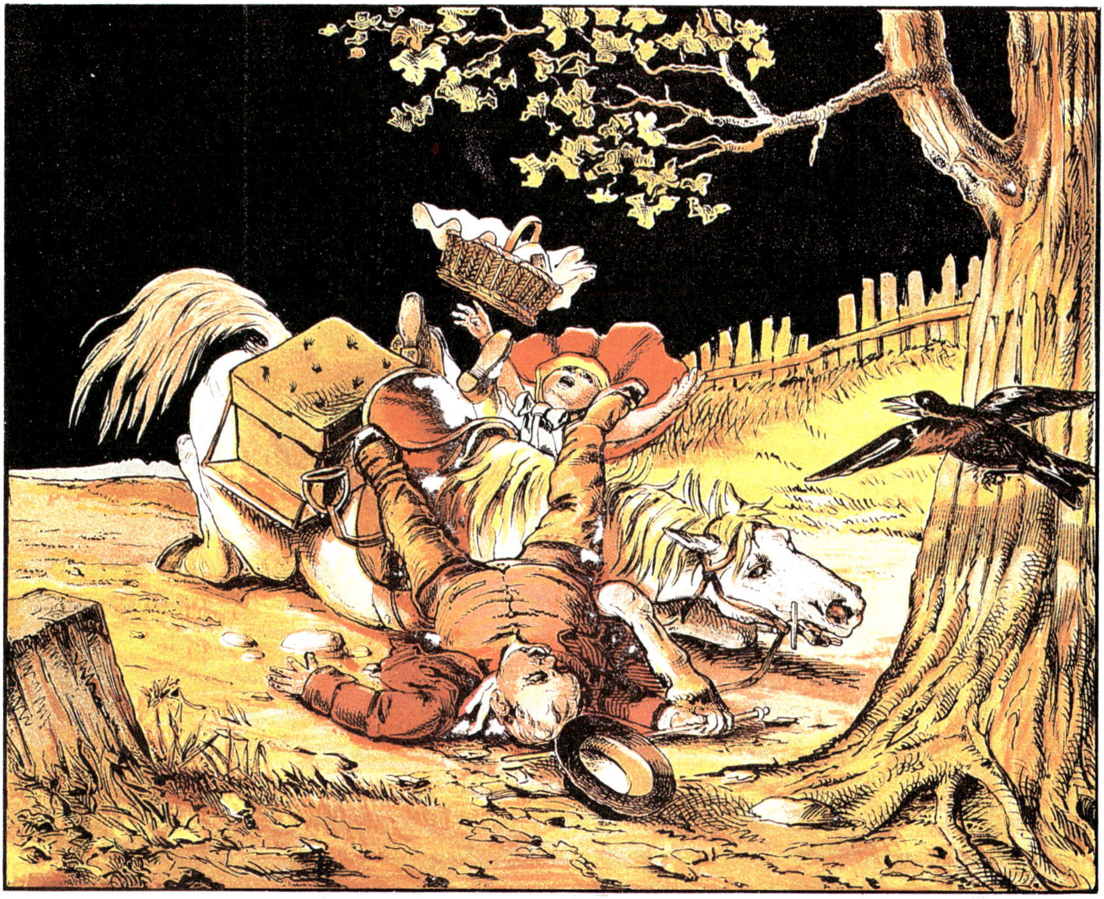

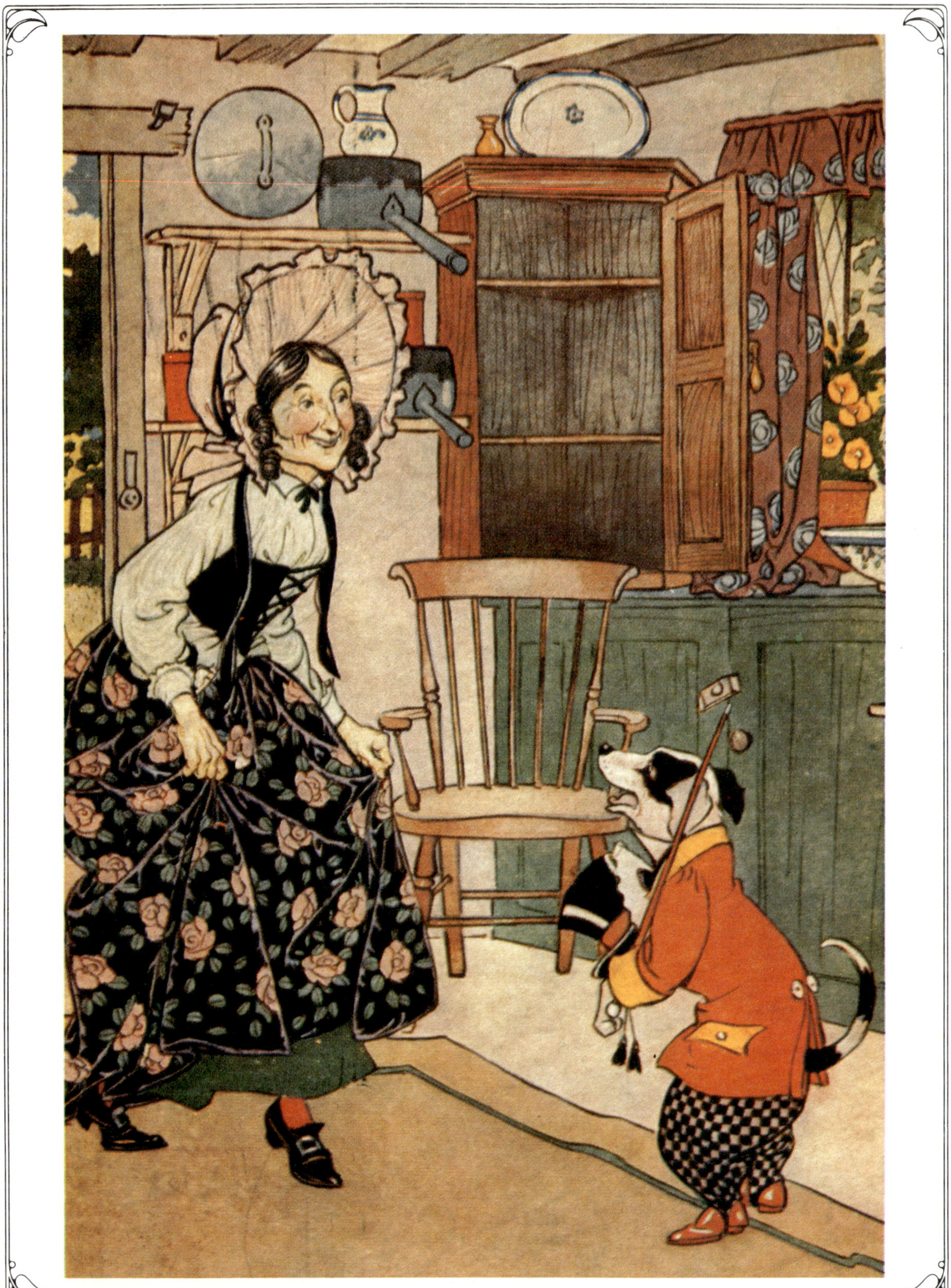

My gal don't wear button-up shoes,
Her feet too big for gaiters,
All she's fit for – a dip of snuff
And a yellow yam potato.

My dog died of whoopin cough,
My mule died of distemper,
Me an' my girl can't git along,
She's got a nasty temper.

You go saddle the old grey mare,
And I'll go plow old muley.
I'll make a turn 'fore the sun goes down,
And I'll go back home to Julie.

Takes four wheels to hold a load,
Takes two mules to pull double,
Take me back to Georgia land
And I won't be any trouble.

Once I had an old grey mare,
And her back wore out and her belly bare.

Then I turned her down the creek,
Purpose of a little green grass to eat.

Then I took her darned old tracks,
And I found her in a mudhole flat of her back.

Then I feeling very stout,
Took her by the tail and I hoist her out.

Then I thought it was no sin,
I hoist up my knife and I skinned her skin.

Then I put in some moose,
Purpose of to make my winter shoes.

Then I hung it in the loft,
'Long come a rogue and stoled it off.

Darn the rogue that stoled it off,
Left my toes all out to the frost.

47

In come de animuls two by two,
Hippopotamus and a kangaroo;
Dem bones gona rise agin.

In come de animuls three by three,
Two big cats and a bumble bee;
Dem bones gona rise agin.

In come de animuls fo' by fo',
Two thru de winder and two thru de do';
Dem bones gona rise agin.

In come de animuls five by five,
Almost dead and hardly alive;
Dem bones gona rise agin.

In come de animuls six by six,
Three wid clubs and three wid sticks;
Dem bones gona rise agin.

In come de animuls seben by seben,
Fo' from Hell and de others from Heaven;
Dem bones gona rise agin.

In come de animuls eight by eight,
Four on time and de others late;
Dem bones gona rise agin.

In come de animuls nine by nine,
Four in front and five behind;
Dem bones gona rise agin.

In come de animuls ten by ten,
Five big roosters and five big hens;
Dem bones gona rise agin.

Says the fly, says he, 'Will you marry me,
And live with me, sweet bumble-bee?'

Said the bee, said she, 'I'll live under your wing.
You'll never know I carry a sting.'

So when the parson beetle joined the pair,
They both went out to take the air.

O, the flies did buzz and the bells did ring.
Did you ever hear so merry a thing?

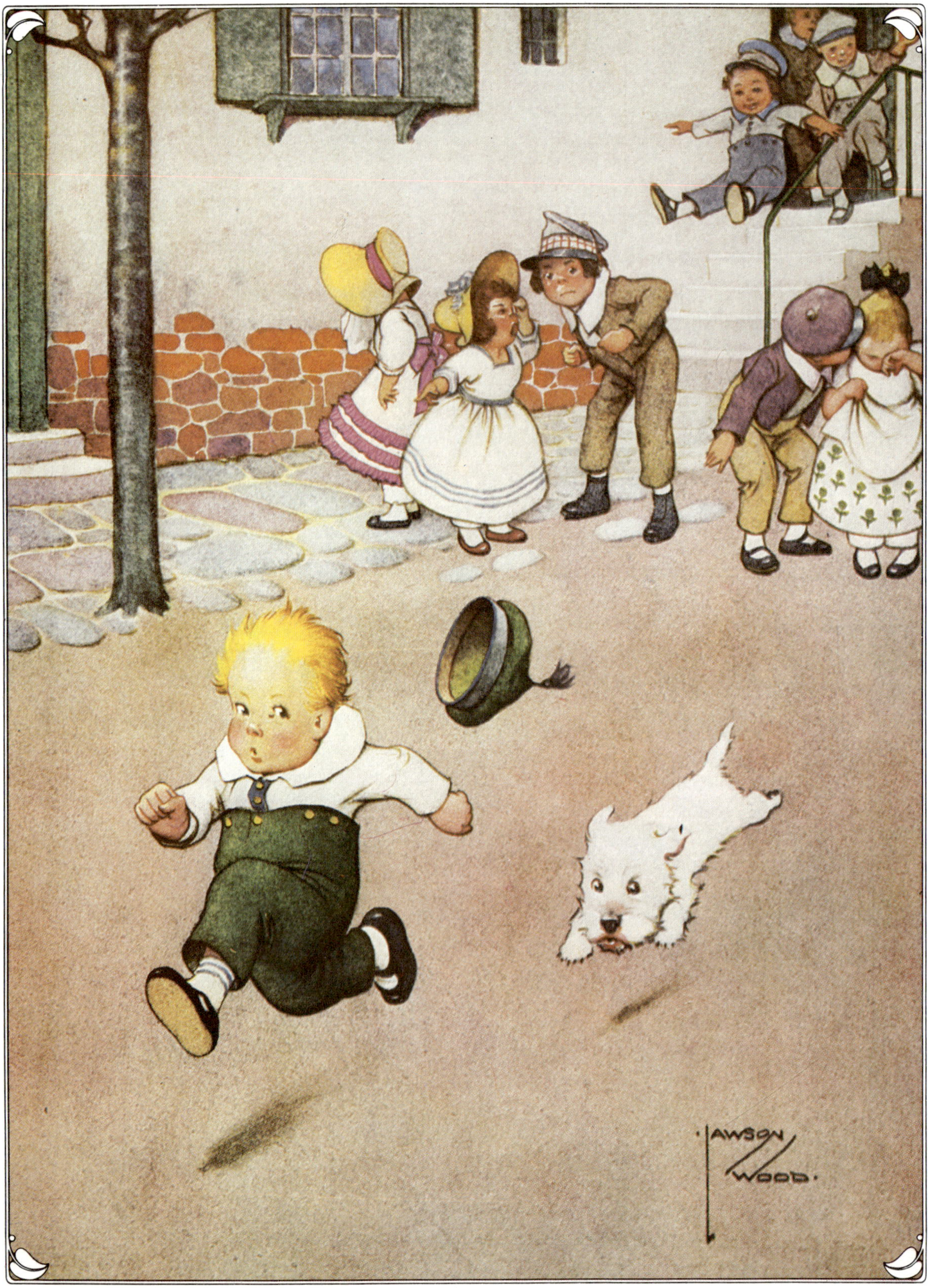
LAWSON WOOD.

Have Fun!

I never went to college,
I never went to school,
But when it comes to boogie
I'm an educated fool.

I went to the river
And couldn't get across,
Paid five dollars
For an old gray hoss.

The horse wouldn't pull,
So I traded for a bull;

The bull wouldn't holler,
So I traded for a dollar;

The dollar wouldn't pass,
So I threw it in the grass;

The grass wouldn't grow,
So I traded for a hoe;

The hoe wouldn't dig,
So I traded for a pig;

The pig wouldn't squeal,
So I traded for a wheel;

The wheel wouldn't run,
So I traded for a gun;

The gun wouldn't shoot,
So I traded for a boot;

The boot wouldn't fit,
So I thought I'd better quit.

When I am president of the United States
I'll eat molasses candy and swing on all the gates.

Pussicat, pussicat, with a white foot,
When is your wedding? for I'll come to't.
The beer's to brew, the bread's to bake,
Pussy-cat, pussy-cat, don't be too late.

Girls and boys come out to play,
The moon doth shine as bright as day.
Leave your supper and leave your sleep,
And join your playfellows in the street.
Come with a whoop and come with a call,
Come with good will or not at all.
Up the ladder and down the wall,
A ha-penny loaf will serve us all;
You find milk, and I'll find flour,
And we'll have a pudding in half an hour.

      A tisket, a tasket,
      Hitler's in his casket;
      Eenie, meenie, Mussolini,
      Six feet underground.

Hitler, Hitler, I've been thinking,
What in the world have you been drinking?
Smells like beer, tastes like wine;
O my gosh, it's turpentine!

      Singing through the forest,
      Rattling over ridges,
      Shooting under arches,
      Running over bridges,
      Whizzing through the mountains,
      Buzzing o'er the vale,

      Bless me! this is pleasant
      A-riding on a rail.
      Singing through the mountains,
      Buzzing o'er the vale,
      Bless me! this is pleasant
      A-riding on a rail.

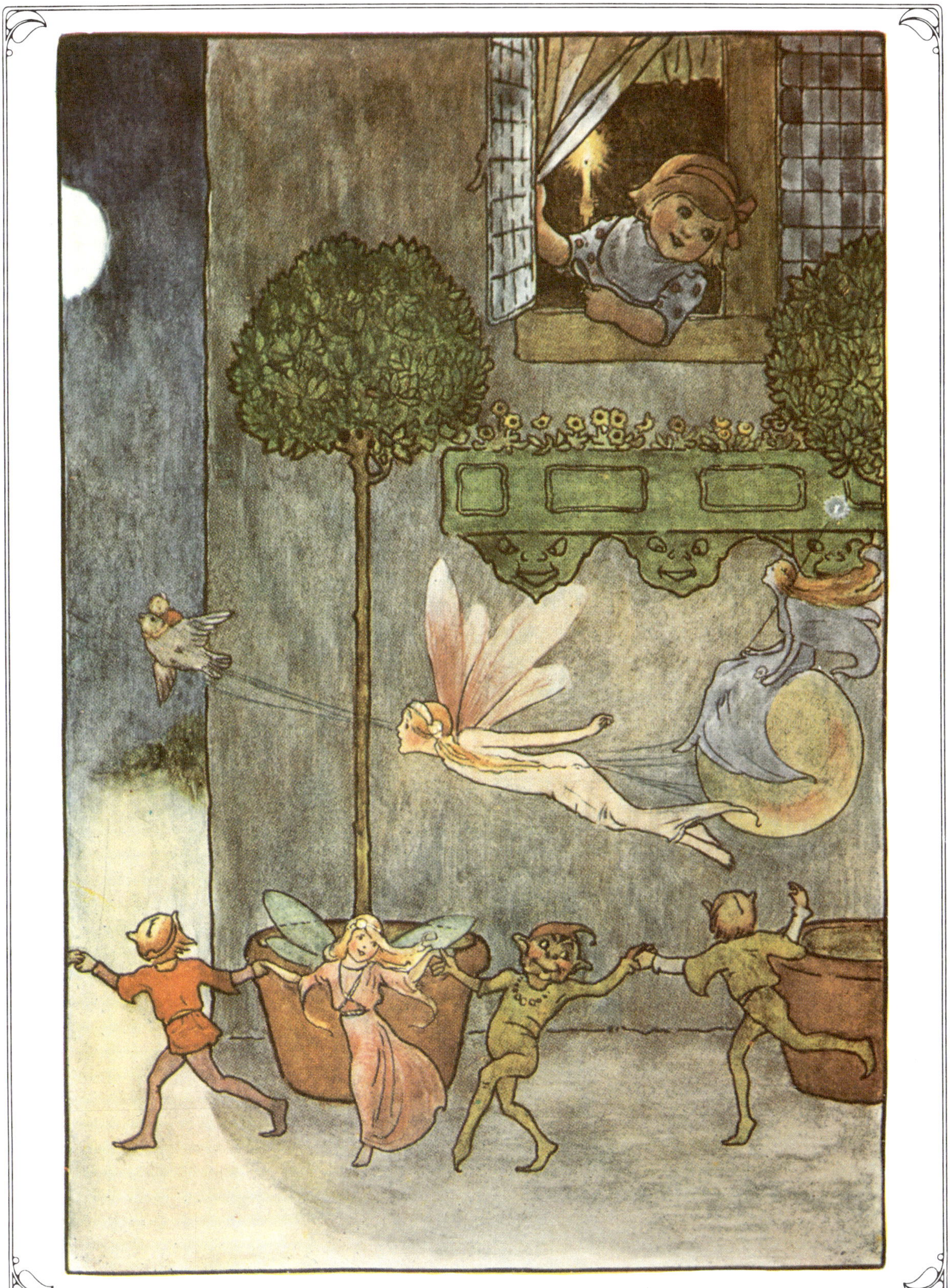

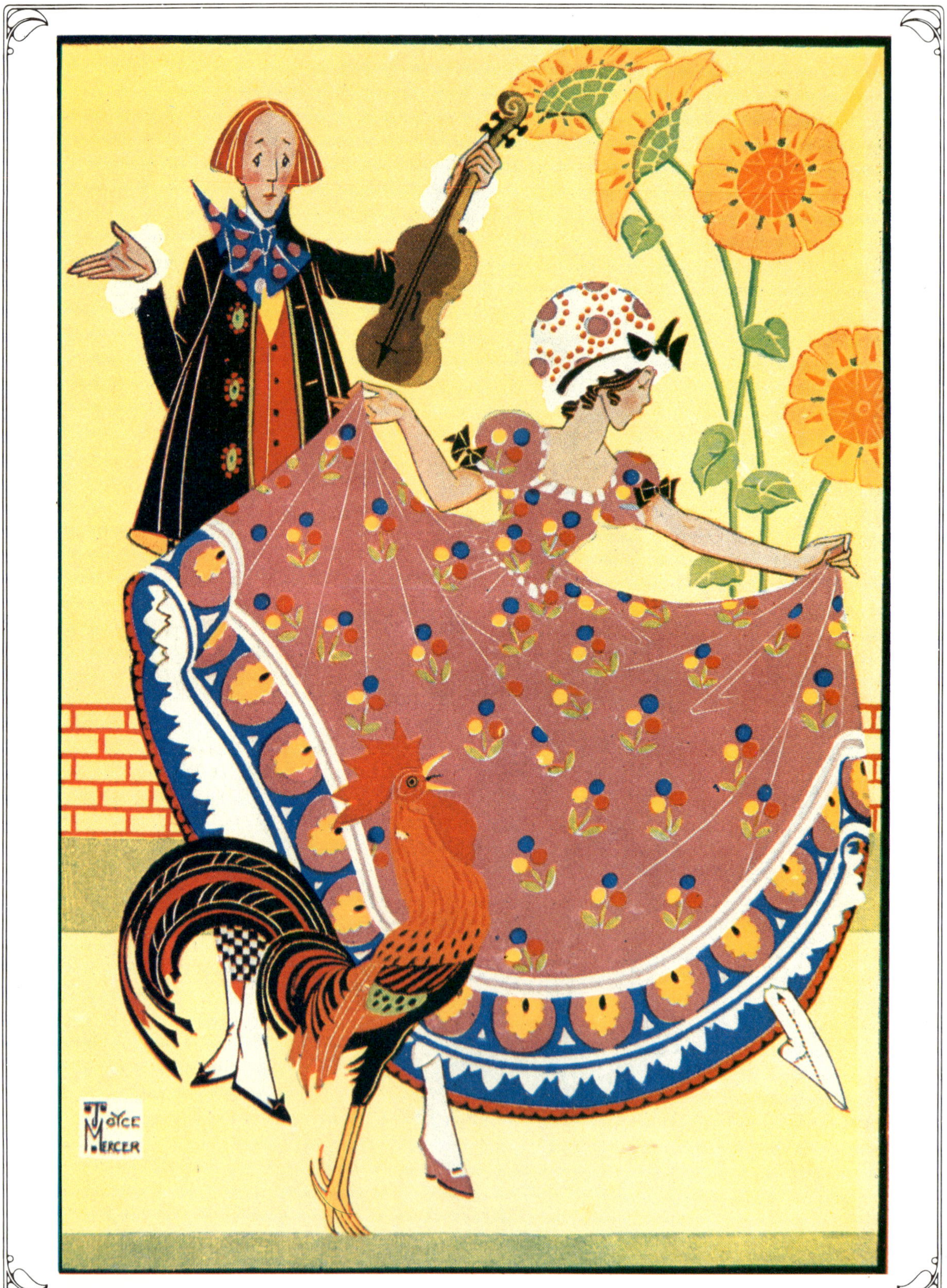
JOYCE
MERCER

I won't be my father's Jack,
I won't be my mother's Jill,
I will be the fiddler's wife,
And have music then I will.

   T'other little tune,
   T'other little tune,
   Prithee, love, play me,
   T'other little tune.

Terence McDiddler,
The three-string fiddler,
Can charm, if you please,
The fish from the seas.

Up the hickory,
Down the pine,
Tore my shirt-tail
Way up behind.

I looked down the road,
Saw Sal a-coming,
Thought to my soul
I'd kill myself a-running.

Monkey in the barnyard,
Monkey in the stable,
Monkey git your hair cut
Soon as you are able.

Had a little pony,
His name was Jack.
Put him in a stable,
And he jumped through a crack.

Chew my tobacco,
And spit my juice,
Want to go to heaven,
But it ain't no use.

There was a monkey climbed a tree,
When he fell down, then down fell he.

There was a crow sat on a stone,
When he was gone, then there was none.

There was an old wife did eat an apple,
When she ate two, she ate a couple.

There was a horse going to the mill,
When he went on, he stood not still.

There was a butcher cut his thumb,
When it did bleed, then blood did come.

There was a lackey ran a race,
When he ran fast, he ran apace.

There was a cobbler clouting shoon,
When they were mended, they were done.

There was a navy went to Spain,
When it returned, it came back again.

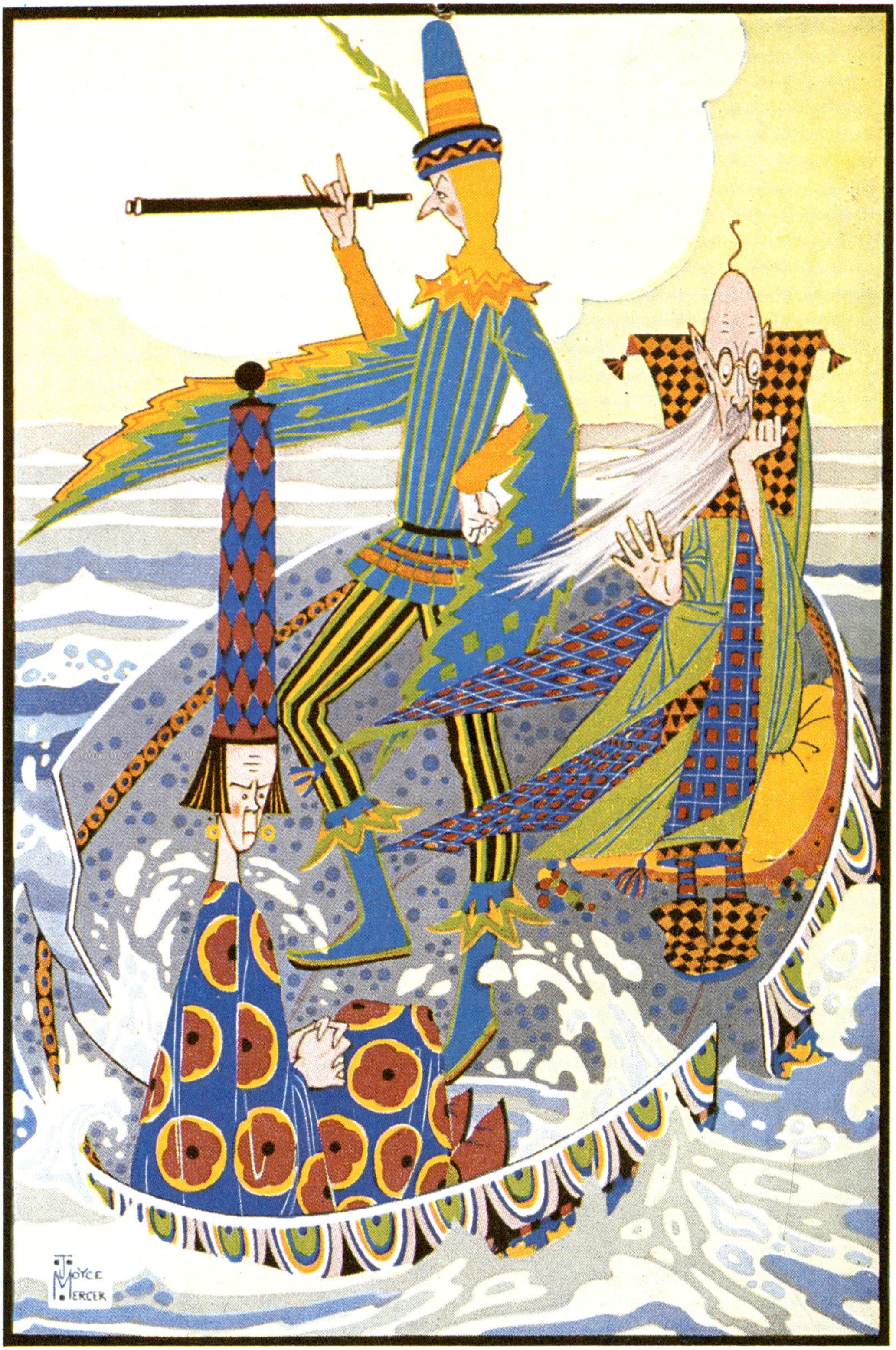
JOYCE MERCER

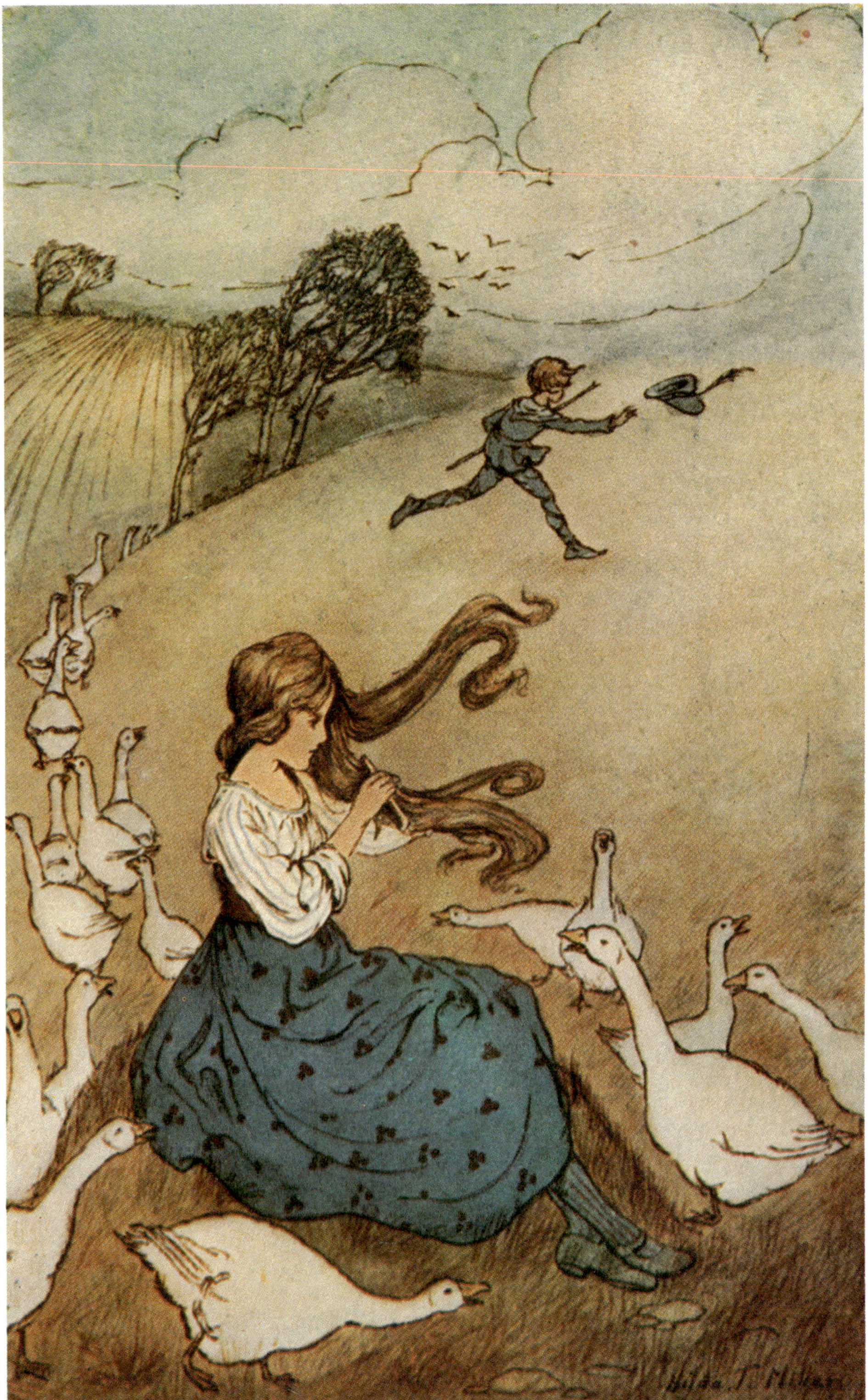
Hilda T. Miller

Ducks in the millpond,
A-geese in the ocean;
A-hug them pretty girls
If I take a notion.

Ducks in the millpond,
A-geese in the clover,
A-jumped in the bed,
And the bed turned over.

Ducks in the millpond,
A-geese in the clover,
A-fell in the millpond,
Wet all over.

My foot in the stirrup, my seat in the saddle,
I'm the best little cowboy that ever rode a-straddle.

I'm on my best horse and I'm going at a run,
I'm the quickest-shooting cowboy that ever pulled a gun.

Oh, my foot's in the stirrup and my hand's on the horn,
I'm the best durn cowboy that ever was born.

With my blankets and my slicker and my rawhide rope,
I'm a-sliding down the trail in a long keen lope.

Oh, a ten-dollar horse and a forty-dollar saddle,
And I'm going to punching Texas cattle.

It's cloudy in the west and looking like rain,
And my darned old slicker's in the wagon again.

I woke up one morning on the old Chisholm Trail
With a rope in my hand and cow by the tail.

My seat in the saddle, and I gave a little shout,
The lead cattle broke and the herd ran about.

I'm up every morning before daylight,
And before I sleep the moon shines bright.

There were three jovial Welshmen, as I have heard them say,
And they would go a-hunting, upon Saint David's day.

All day they hunted and nothing could they find,
But a ship a-sailing, and that they left behind.

One said it was a ship, the other he said 'Nay!'
The third said it was a house with the chimney blown away.

All the night they hunted and nothing could they find,
But the moon a-gliding and that they left behind.

One said it was the moon, the other he said 'Nay!'
The third said it was a cheese with half o't cut away.

And all day they hunted and nothing could they find,
But a hedgehog in a bramble-bush, and that they left behind.

The first said it was a hedgehog, the second he said 'Nay!'
The third said it was a pin-cushion with the pins stuck in wrong way.

And all night they hunted and nothing could they find,
But an owl in a holly tree, and that they left behind.

One said it was an owl, the other he say 'Nay!'
The third said it was an old man, and his beard growing grey.

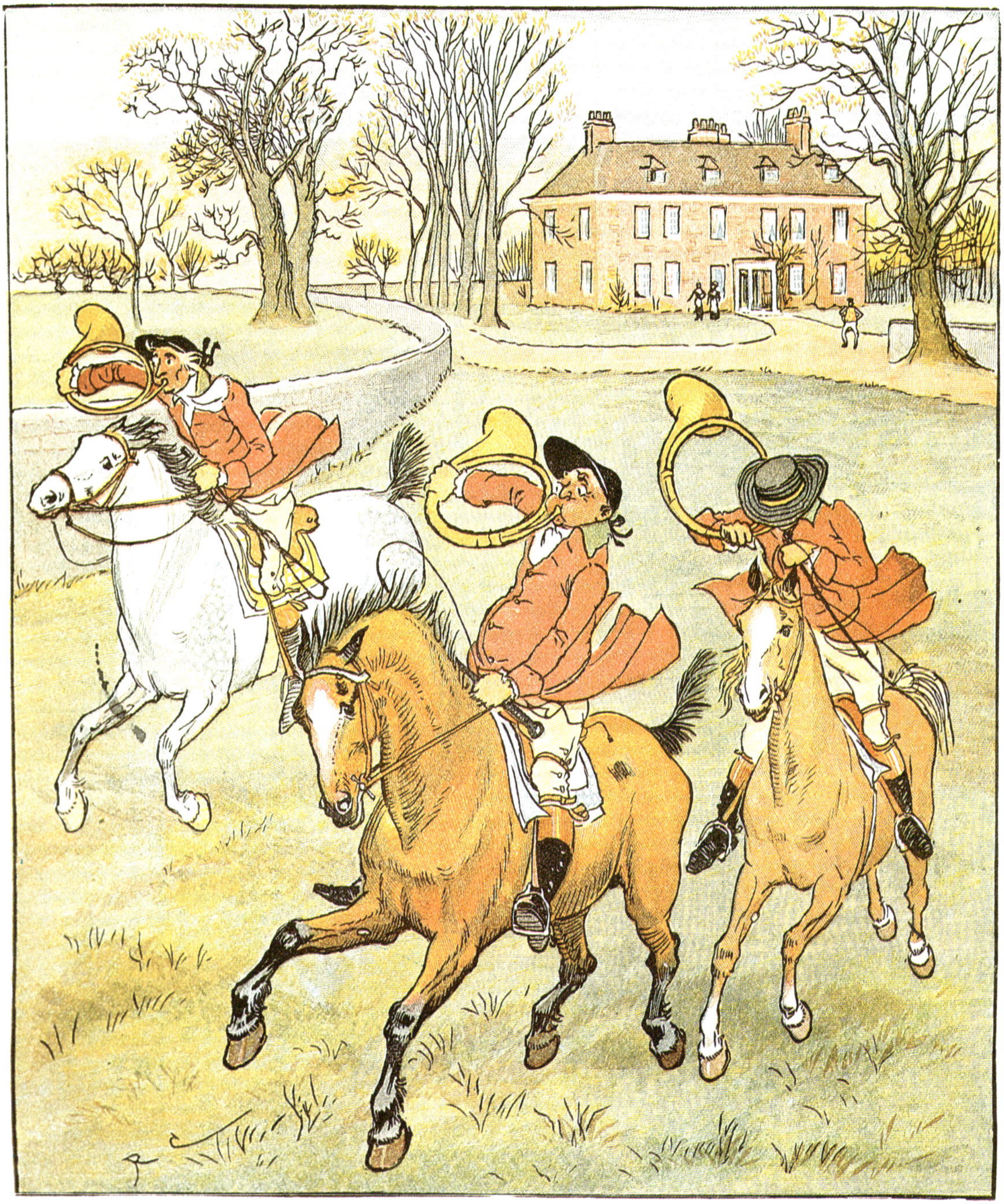

Dancing Dolly has no sense;
She bought a fiddle for 18 pence.
But the only tune that she could play
Was 'Sally, get out of the Donkey's way'.

Lawd-a-mercy, what have you done?
You've married the old man instead of his son!
His legs are all crooked and wrong put on,
They're all a-laughing at your old man.

Now you're married you must obey.
You must prove true to all you say.
And as you have promised, so now you must do, –
Kiss him twice and hug him, too.

Old Father Long-legs
Can't say his prayers;
Take him by the left leg
And throw him down stairs.
And when he's at the bottom,
Before he long has lain,
Take him by the right leg,
And throw him up again.

Hey diddle diddle,
The cat and the fiddle,
The cow jumped over the moon;
The little dog laughed
To see such sport,
And the dish ran away with the spoon.

This pig went to market;
This pig stayed at home;
This pig had a bit of meat;
And this pig had none;
This pig said, Wee, wee, wee!
I can't find my way home.

Old woman, old woman, will you go a-shearing?
Speak a little louder, sir, I'm rather hard of hearing.
Old woman, old woman, are you good at weaving?
Pray speak a little louder sir, my hearing is deceiving.

Old woman, old woman, will you go a-walking?
Speak a little louder, sir, or what's the good of talking.
Old woman, old woman, are you fond of spinning?
Pray speak a little louder sir, I only see you grinning.

Old woman, old woman, will you do my knitting?
My hearing's getting better now. Come nearer where
   I'm sitting.
Old woman, old woman, shall I kiss you dearly?
O Lawdamercy on my soul, now I hear you clearly!

Humpty Dumpty

Take Heed!

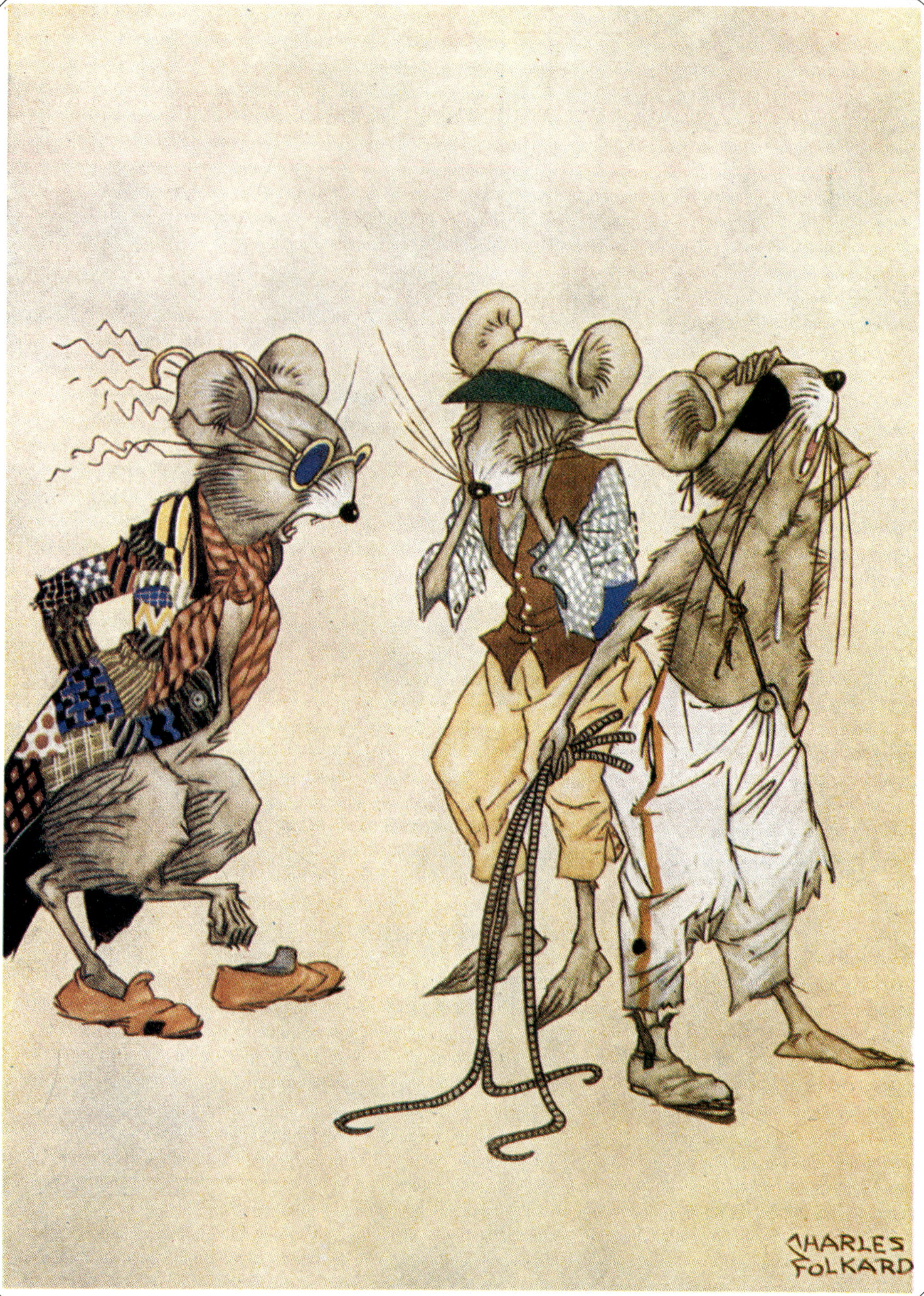
CHARLES
FOLKARD

Three blind mice, see how they run!
They all ran after the farmer's wife,
Who cut off their tails with a carving knife,
Did you ever see such a thing in your life,
As three blind mice.

Come, let's to bed, says Sleepy-head;
   Sit up awhile, says Slow.
Hang on the pot, say Greedy Gut,
   We'll sup before we go.

To bed, to bed, cries Sleepy-head,
   But all the rest said, No.
It's morning now, you must milk the cow,
   And tomorrow to bed we go.

Reader, behold! this monster wild
Has gobbled up the infant child.
The infant child is not aware
It has been eaten by the bear.

Tom tied a kettle to the tail of a cat,
Jill put a stone in a blindman's hat,
Bob threw his grandmother down the stairs:
They all grew up ugly, and nobody cares.

A red cockatoo.
Coloured like the peach-tree blossom,
Speaking with the speech of men.
And they did to it what is always done
To the learned and eloquent.
They took a cage with stout bars
And shut it up inside.

I sold me a horse
   And bought me a cow,
I tried to make bargains
   But didn't know how.

I sold me a cow
   And bought me a calf,
I tried to make bargains
   But always lost half.

I sold me a calf
   And bought me a swine,
He couldn't chew corn,
   For his teeth were too fine.

I sold me a swine
   And bought me a hen,
She laid eggs,
   But the devil knew when.

I sold me a hen
   And bought me a cock,
He never crowed
   Till 9 o'clock.

I sold me a cock
   And bought me a rat,
His tail caught a-fire,
   And burned my old hat.

   I sold me a rat
      And bought me a mouse,
   His tail caught on fire
      And burned my old house.

I was standing on the corner
Not doing any harm,
Along came a policeman
And took me by the arm.
He took me round the corner
And rang a little bell,
Along came a police car
And took me to a cell.

I woke in the morning
And looked up on the wall.
The cooties and the bedbugs
Were having a game of ball.
The score was six to nothing,
The bedbugs were ahead.
The cooties hit a home run
And knocked me out of bed.

When the farmer comes to town,
With his wagon broken down,
O, the farmer is the man who feeds them all!
If you'll only look and see,
I think you will agree
That the farmer is the man who feeds them all.

The doctor hangs around
While the blacksmith heats his iron,
O, the farmer is the man who feeds them all!
The preacher and the cook
Go strolling by the brook,
And the farmer is the man who feeds them all.

The farmer is the man,
The farmer is the man,
Buys on credit till the fall.
Tho' his family comes to town,
With a wagon broken down,
O, the farmer is the man who feeds them all!

The rich man lay on his velvet couch,
   He ate from plates of gold;
A poor girl stood on the marble step,
   And cried, 'So cold, so cold!'

Three years went by and the rich man died;
   He descended to fiery hell;
The poor girl lay in an angel's arms
   And sighed, 'All's well – all's well!'

'Twixt Handkerchief and Nose
A difference arose;
And a tradition goes
That they settled it by blows.

I think that I shall never see
A billboard lovely as a tree.
Indeed, unless the billboards fall
I'll never see a tree at all.

The big bee flies high
The little bee makes the honey.
The black folks make the cotton
And the white folks get the money.

Johnny on the railroad, picking up stones,
Along came an engine and broke Johnny's bones.
'O,' said Johnny, 'that's not fair.'
'O,' said the driver, 'I don't care.'

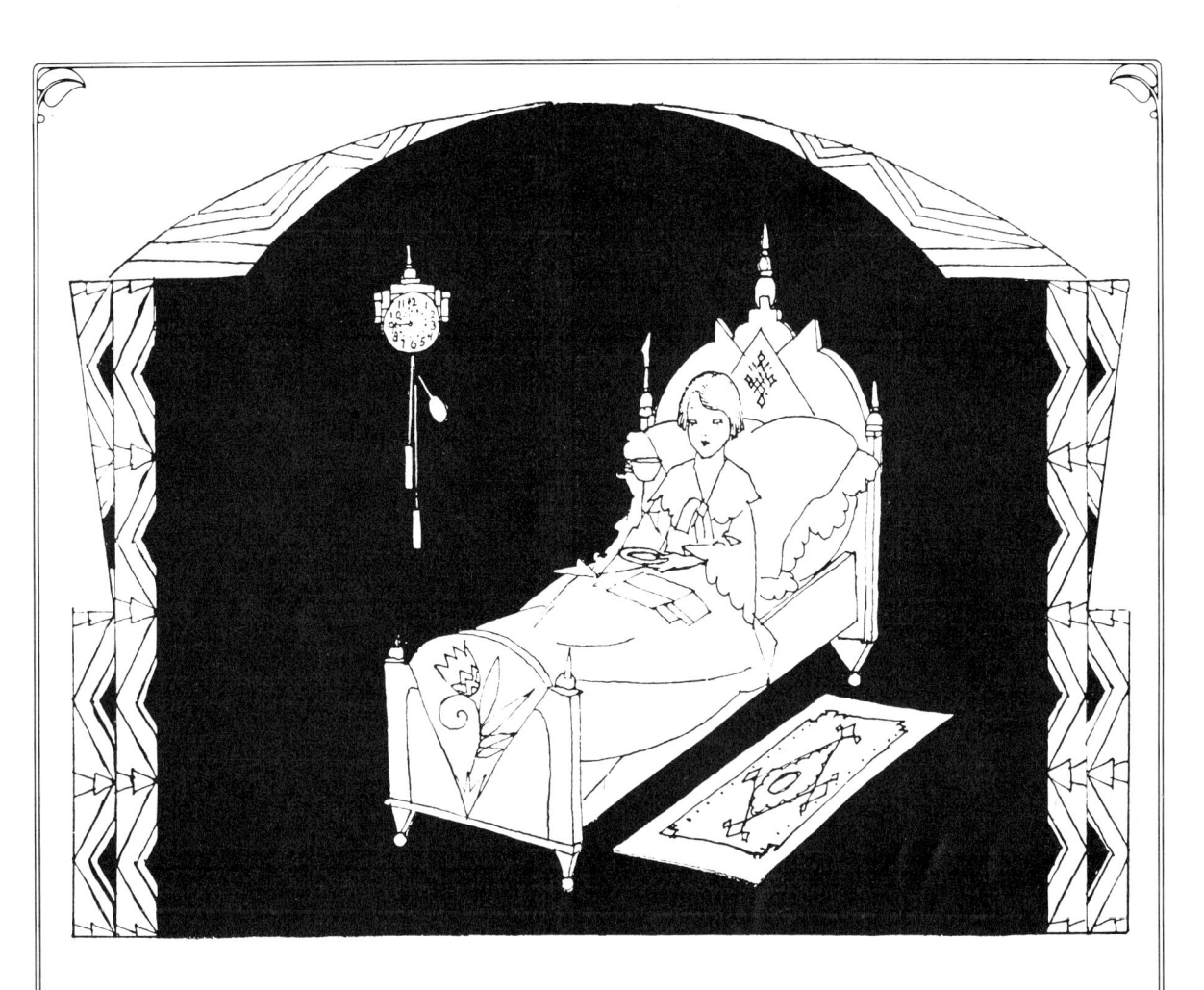

O money is the meat in the cocoanut,
O money is the milk in the jug;
When you've got lots of money
You feel very funny,
You're as happy as a bug in a rug.

My father died a month ago,
He left me all his riches –
A feather bed and a wooden leg,
And a pair of leather breeches;
A coffee pot without a spout,
A cup without a handle,
A baccy box without a lid,
And half a ha'penny candle.

See-saw, Margery Daw.
Jacky shall have a new master;
Jacky shall have but a penny a day,
Because he can't work any faster.

I'll eat when I'm hungry
And drink when I'm dry.
If a tree don't fall on me
I'll live till I die.

There was an old woman who lived in a shoe,
She had so many children she didn't know what to do;
She gave them some broth without any bread;
She whipped them all soundly and put them to bed.

The Old Woman Who Lived in a Shoe

Index of First Lines

A hungry fox one day did spy, 36
All I need to make me happy, 14
A red cockatoo, 73 (Arthur Waley)
A tisket, a tasket, 54
A tumbled down, and hurt his Arm, against a bit of wood, 21

Baa, baa, black sheep, 26

Chicken in the bread-pan, 14
Come, let's to bed, says Sleepy-head, 73

Daddy shot a bear, 38
Dancing Dolly has no sense, 64
Ducks in the millpond, 61

Five little monkeys walked along the shore, 32
Flies in the buttermilk, two by two, 28
Four and twenty tailor lads, 37

Girls and boys come out to play, 54
Girls are dandy, 27

Hey diddle diddle, 67
Hickory, dickory dock, 25
Hitler, Hitler, I've been thinking, 54

I brought my love a cherry that has no stone, 18
I dreamed that my horse had wings and could fly, 33
I'll eat when I'm hungry, 78
I'm goin' away to stay a little while, 13
I'm so sorry for old Adam, 11
In come de animuls two by two, 48
I never went to college, 52
I sold me a horse, 74
I think that I shall never see, 76 (Ogden Nash)
I was standing on the corner, 75
I went to the river, 52
I WISH I were a, 35
I won't be my father's Jack, 57

Johnny on the railroad, picking up stones, 76

Lawd a-mercy, what have you done?, 65
Little Betty Winkle she had a pig, 40
Little Jack Horner, 28
London Bridge is falling down, 16

Massah had an old black mule, 32
Mister Rabbit, Mister Rabbit, your ears mighty long, 41
My father died a month ago, 77
My foot in the stirrup my seat in the saddle, 61

My gal don't wear button-up shoes, 45
My Mammy was a wall-eyed goat, 34
My sweetheart's a mule in the mines, 37

Old Father Long-legs, 66
Old Mistress McShuttle, 39
Old woman, old woman, will you go a-shearing, 69
Ol Mr Rabbit, 38
O money is the meat in the cocoanut, 77
Once I had an old grey mare, 46
Our dog Fred, 38 (James Whitcomb Riley)

Pussicat, pussicat, with a white foot, 53

Reader, behold! this monster wild, 73 (A. E. Housman)
Ring-a-ring o' roses, 24

Says the fly, says he, 'will you marry me', 49
See-saw, Margery Daw, 78
Singing through the forest, 54
Sleep, baby, sleep, 10

Terence McDiddler, 57
The big bee flies high, 76
The Kitty-Cat Bird, he sat on a Fence, 42 (Theodore Roethke)
The Lord made an elephant, 32
The panther is like a leopard, 36 (Ogden Nash)
There was a little turtle, 36 (Vachel Lindsay)
There was a monkey climbed a tree, 58
There was an Old Woman, 14
There was an old woman who lived in a shoe, 78
There were three jovial Welshmen, as I have heard them say, 62
The rich man lay on his velvet couch, 76
This pig went to market, 68
Three blind mice, see how they run!, 73
Three children sliding on the ice, 19
Three mice went into a hole to spin, 34
Tom tied a kettle to the tail of a cat, 73
'Twixt Handkerchief and Nose, 76 (John B. Tabb)

Up the hickory, 57

We dance round in a ring and suppose, 11 (Robert Frost)
What is there hid in the heart of a rose, 12 (Alfred Noyes)
When I am president of the United States, 52
When the farmer comes to town, 75
'Who's that tickling my back?' said the wall, 36 (Ian Seraillier)

Young lambs to sell, 14

Index of Artists

Adams, Frank 47
Anderson, Anne 64
Brooke, Leslie 68
Browne, Gordon 38
Caldecott, Randolph 39, 48, 63, 74
Edgerton, Linda 12, 13, 27
Folkard, Charles 72
Greenaway, Kate 24
Jackson, Helen 53
Kidd, Will 40
Le Mair, Willebeck 15, 16, 18
Mercer, Joyce 56, 59
Miller, Hilda T. 60
Pierce, Susan 41
Pogany, Willy 10, 37, 77
Rackham, Arthur 67
Sowerby, Millicent 55
Wanke, Alice 29
Watson, A. H. 66
Wheeler, Dorothy 2
Wood, Lawson 25, 50